DISCOVERING MAPS

Floor Plans

Harriet Brundle
and John Willis

AV2
www.openlightbox.com

AV2

Step 1
Go to **www.openlightbox.com**

Step 2
Enter this unique code
MUGNH6MWH

Step 3
Explore your interactive eBook!

AV2 is optimized for use on any device

Your interactive eBook comes with...

- **Audio** – Listen to the entire book read aloud
- **Videos** – Watch informative video clips
- **Weblinks** – Gain additional information for research
- **Try This!** – Complete activities and hands-on experiments
- **Key Words** – Study vocabulary, and complete a matching word activity
- **Quizzes** – Test your knowledge
- **Slideshows** – View images and captions
- **Share** – Share titles within your Learning Management System (LMS) or Library Circulation System
- **Citation** – Create bibliographical references following APA, CMOS, and MLA styles

This title is part of our AV2 digital subscription

1-Year K–5 Subscription
ISBN 978-1-7911-3320-7

Access hundreds of AV2 titles with our digital subscription.
Sign up for a FREE trial at **www.openlightbox.com/trial**

The digital components of this book are guaranteed to stay active for at least five years from the date of publication.

DISCOVERING MAPS

Floor Plans

CONTENTS

What Is a Map?

A map is a picture that gives people information about an area. Maps can show many different things, such as roads, population, or weather.

A map can be on paper or digital, which means it is on a screen.

Paper or Digital?

Paper Maps

The information in paper maps does not change. They can be used without needing electricity.

Digital Maps

The information in digital maps can be updated. An electronic device is needed to use them.

Using a Map

Maps have colors or symbols to represent different things.

A symbol on a map might show where a school is.

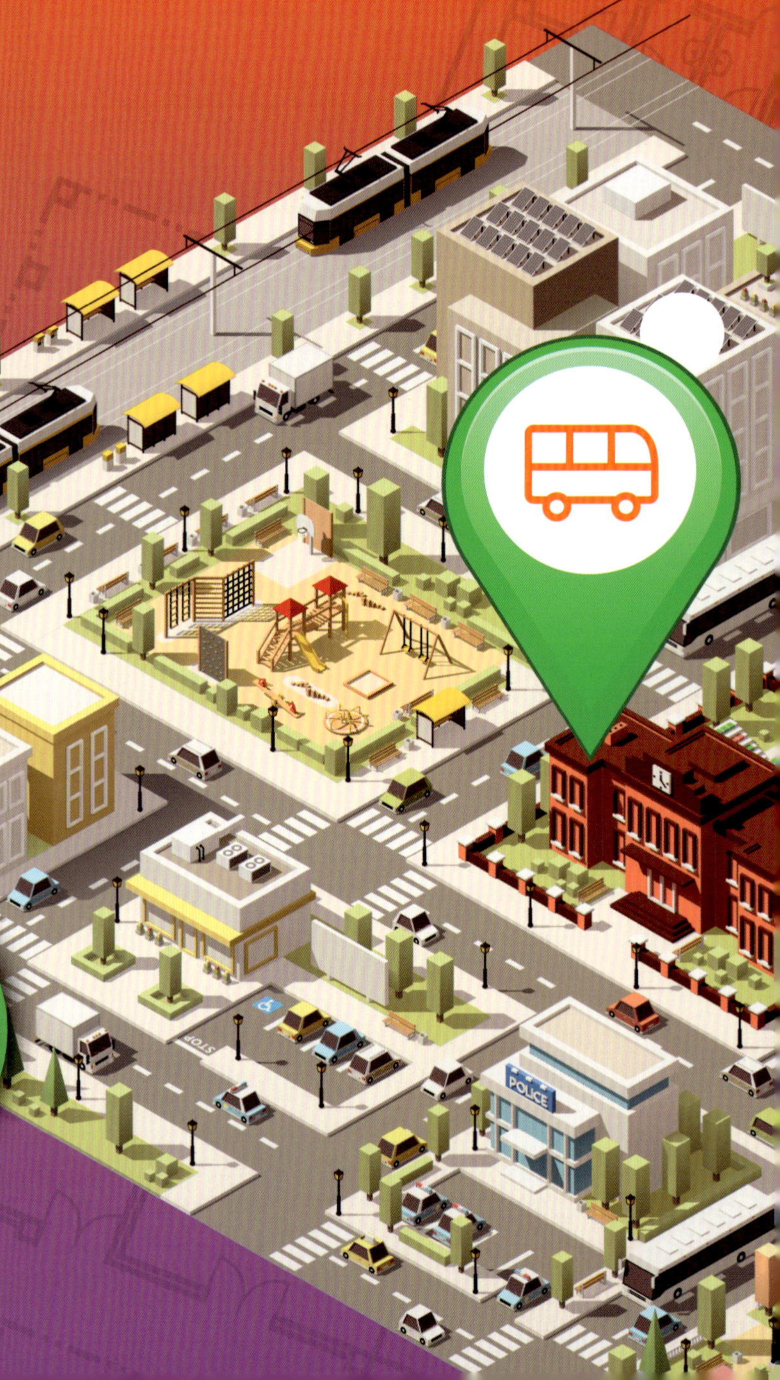

The Boston Latin School was founded on April 23, 1635. It is the oldest public school in the United States.

Map Key

Often, the symbols on a map look like what they represent. A map key can be used to check what the symbols mean.

Most maps are drawn from a "bird's-eye view." This means that they show what a place looks like from above.

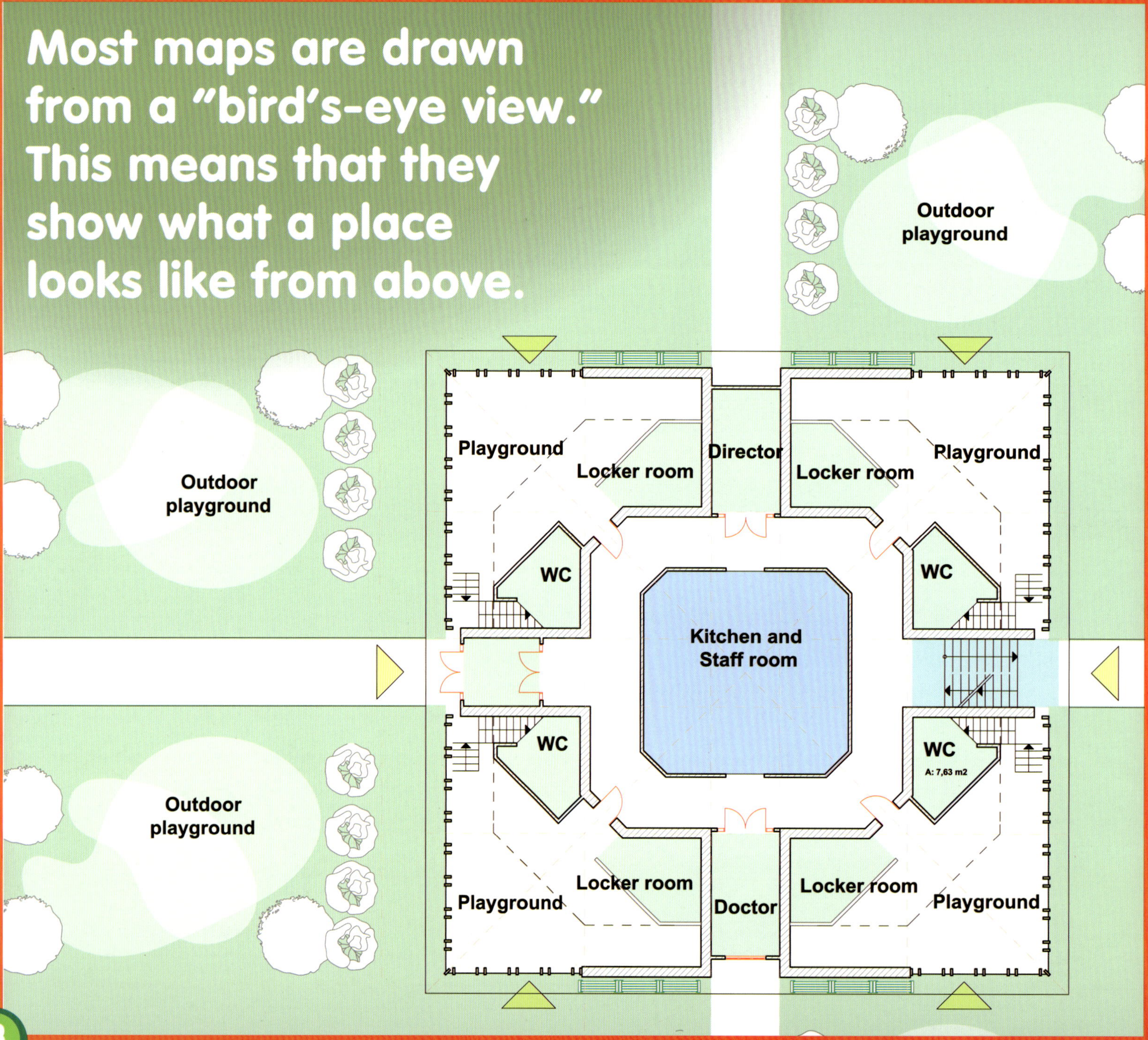

Maps often have a compass printed on them. It shows which way on the map is north, south, east, or west.

Scale

Everything on a map has been made smaller, or "scaled down," to fit.

The amount by which something is made smaller is called the scale.

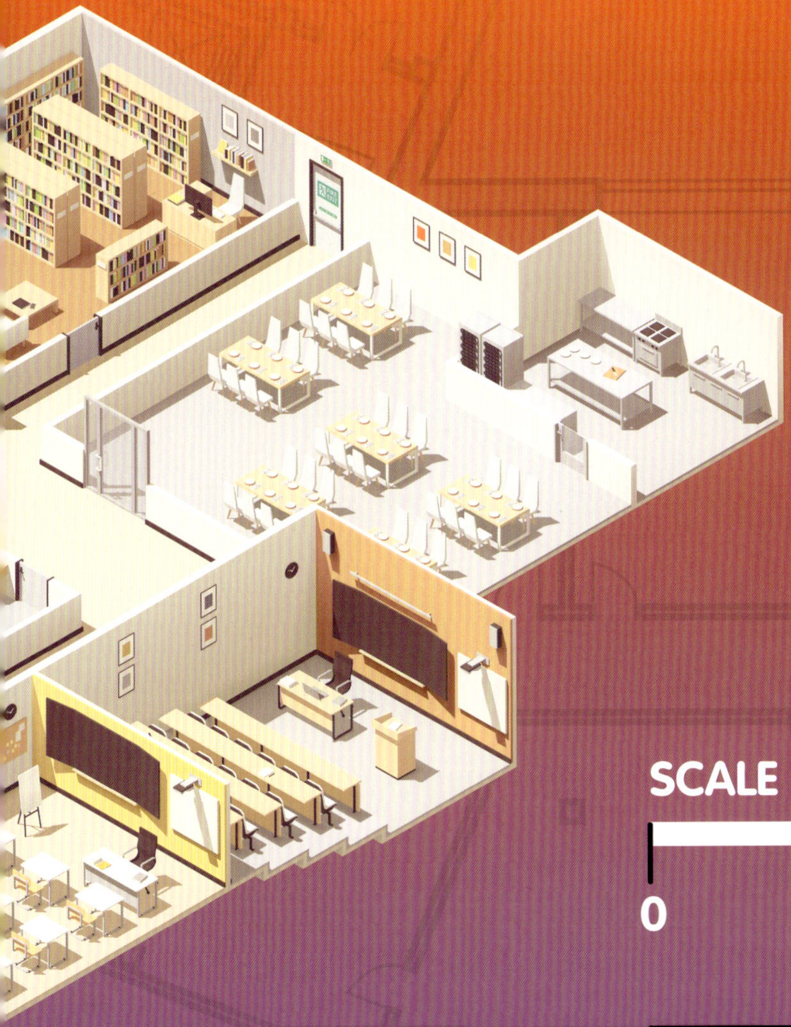

A scale means people can use a map to show distance. If someone wants to know how big a room is, they can use a map scale.

Different Maps

There are many different types of maps.

Physical maps show the features of a place, such as rivers or mountains.

Road maps show all the roads in an area. They also show points of interest. These are locations that people may find useful.

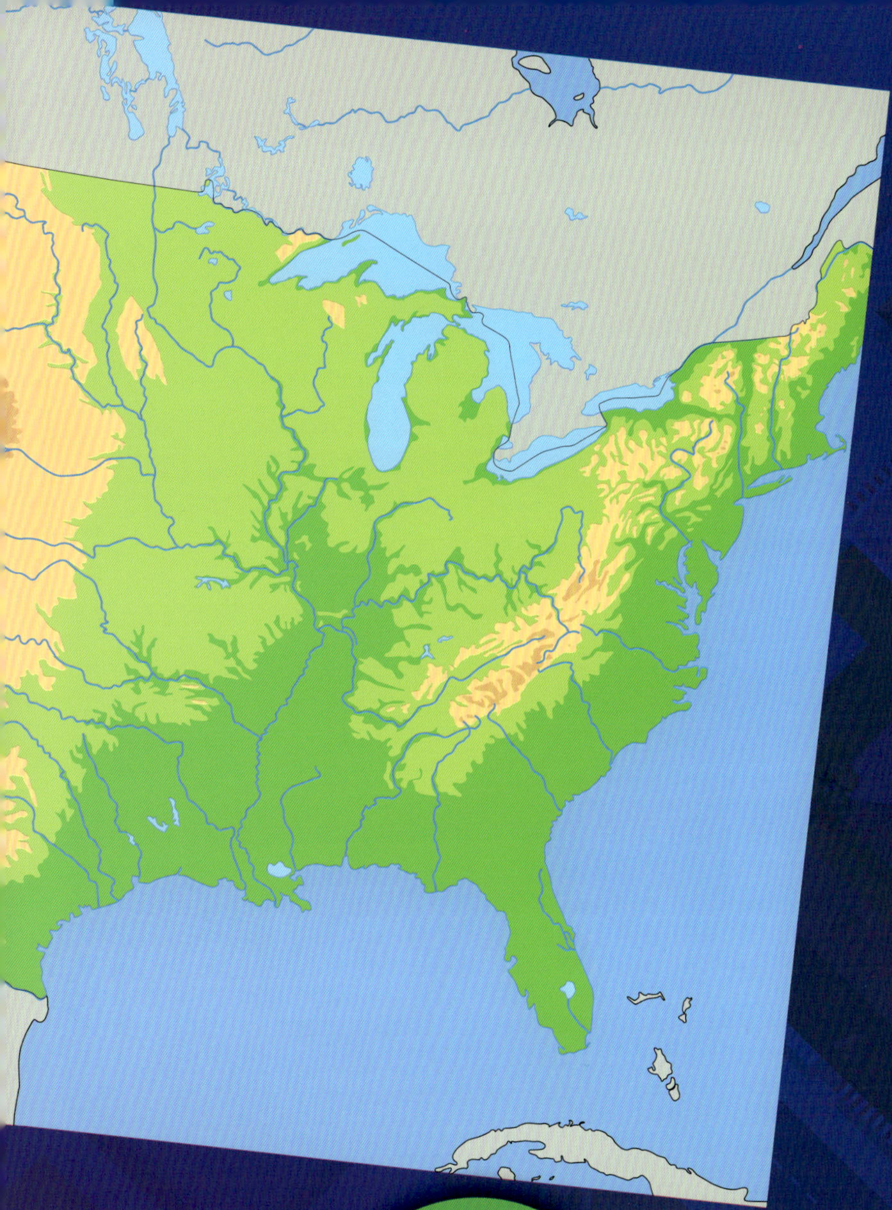

Building maps show the layout of a building. They help people find their way around.

Building maps are often found in malls and other stores. They can help customers find certain shops or products.

How is a Map Made?

To make a map, all the important information must be researched first. This can include the location of any points of interest.

Next, the different parts of a map are filled in step-by-step according to the type of map being created.

Floor Plans

To show the layout of a building, people can look at a type of map called a floor plan.

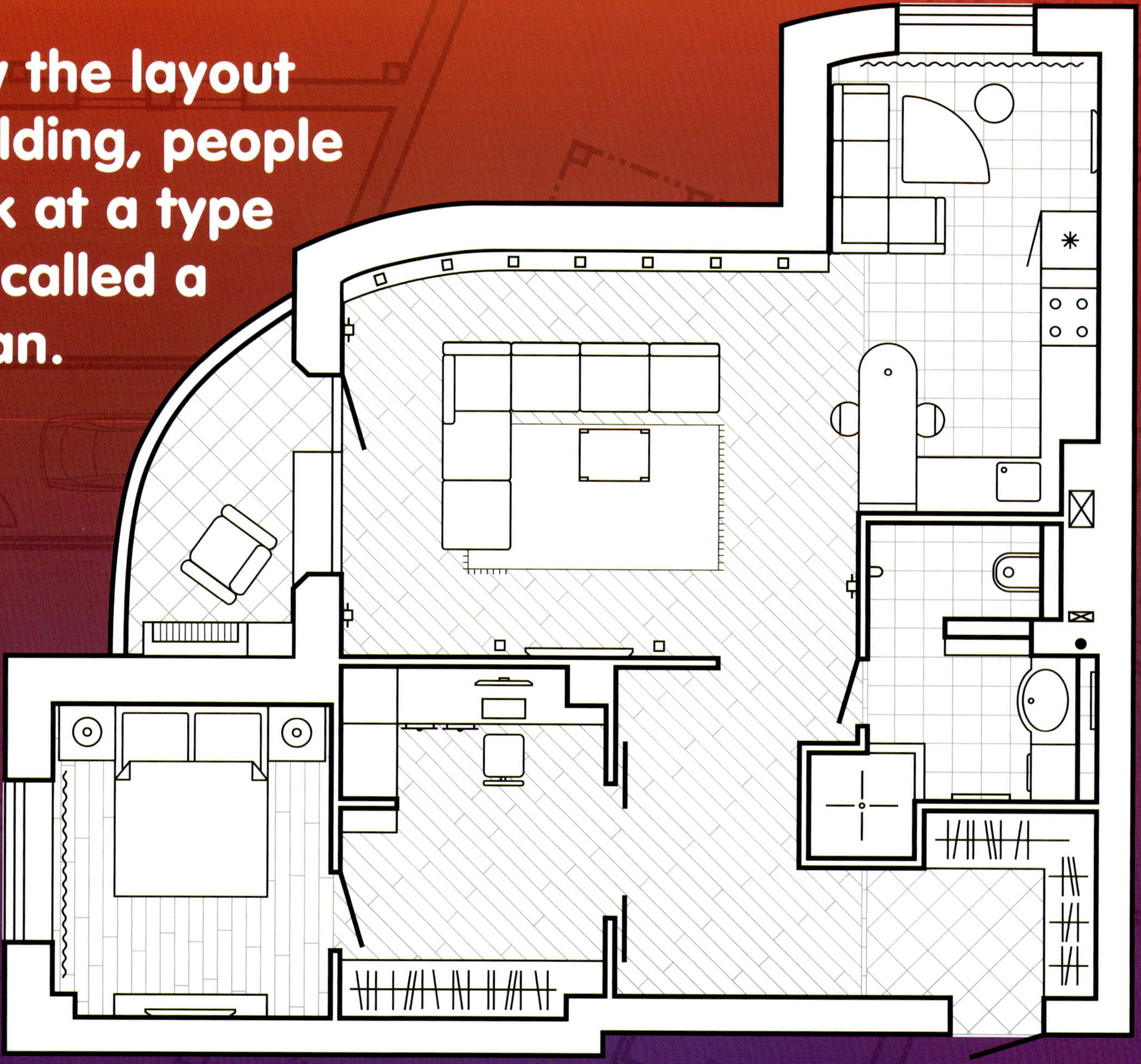

Floor plans are drawn in bird's-eye view. They show how different rooms link together inside a building.

Mapping Your School

STEP 1 – POINTS OF INTEREST

The first step to mapping your school is to make a list of all the points of interest. In school, these may include classrooms, the library, reception, the cafeteria, and the gym.

STEP 2 – CREATE A KEY

Next, create symbols for each point of interest. Then, you can make a key for your map.

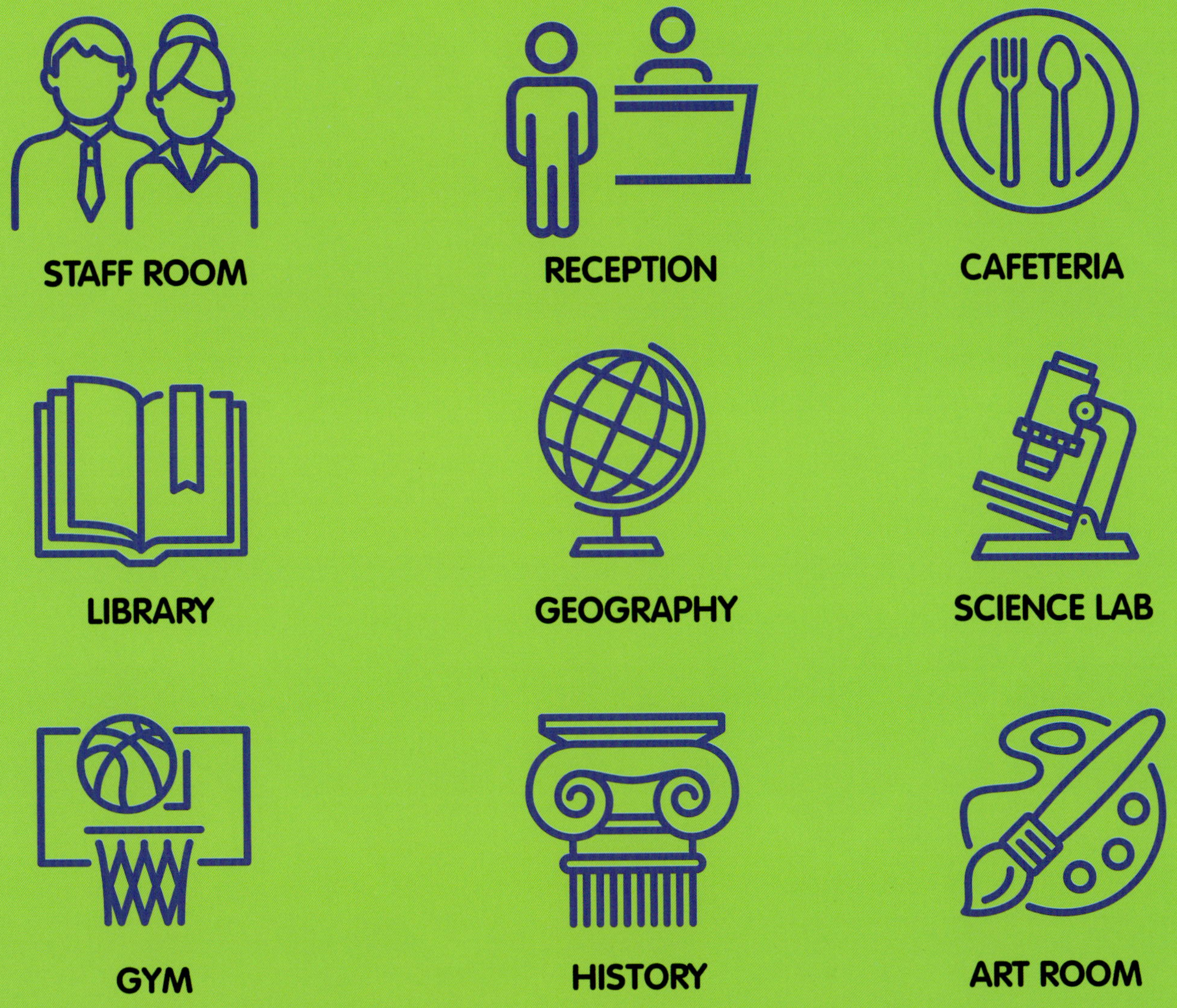

STEP 3 – DRAW YOUR FLOOR PLAN

Imagine your school as if you were looking at it from above. Start by drawing the outline of your school.

STEP 4 – ADD THE DETAILS

Draw the walls of the rooms in your school. Add labels to show what each room is.

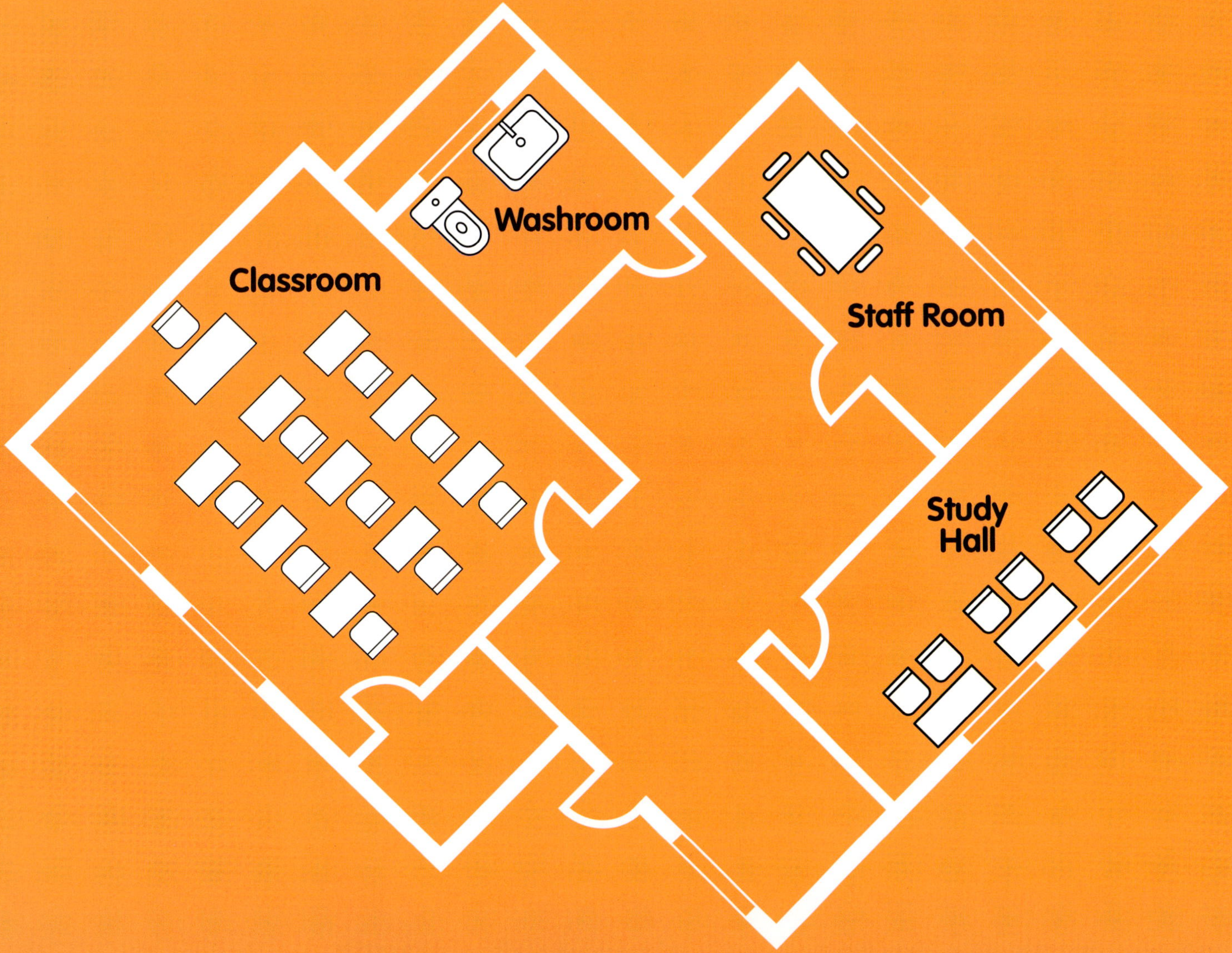

Be Creative!

Use a floor plan to create a school of your own design. Start by thinking about all the different points of interest you want include. Next, you need to make a key.

Then, draw the floor plan of your school. What shape would the building be? Fill in all the different rooms to create the floor plan.

KEY WORDS

Research has shown that as much as 65 percent of all written material published in English is made up of 300 words. These 300 words cannot be taught using pictures or learned by sounding them out. They must be recognized by sight. This book contains 97 common sight words to help young readers improve their reading fluency and comprehension. This book also teaches young readers several important content words, such as proper nouns.

Page	Sight Words First Appearance
4	a, about, an, as, be, can, different, gives, is, it, many, means, on, or, paper, people, picture, show, such, that, things, what, which
5	change, does, in, not, the, them, they, to, use, without
6	have, might, school, states, was, where
7	like, look, often
8	above, are, eye, from, most, place, this
9	way
10	been, by, down, feet, has, made, something
11	big, how, if, know, no, wants
12	all, also, find, may, mountains, of, points, rivers, there, these
13	around, help, other, their
14	any, first, important, make, must
15	being, next, parts
16	at
17	together
18	and, list, your
19	each, for, then, you
20	start, were
21	add

Page	Content Words First Appearance
4	area, information, map, population, roads, screen, weather
5	device, electricity
6	Boston Latin School, colors, symbols, United States
7	classroom, gym, key, laboratory, library, washrooms
8	view
9	compass
10	amount, scale
11	distance, room
12	features, locations, types
13	building, customers, layout, malls, products, shops, stores
16	floor plan
18	cafeteria, reception, step
19	art room, geography, history, science lab, staff room
20	outline
21	details, labels, walls

Published by Lightbox Learning Inc.
276 5th Avenue, Suite 704 #917
New York, NY 10001
Website: www.openlightbox.com

Library of Congress Control Number available upon request.

ISBN 978-1-5105-6353-7 (hardcover)
ISBN 979-8-8745-1506-5 (softcover)
ISBN 978-1-5105-6354-4 (static multi-user eBook)
ISBN 978-1-5105-8145-6 (interactive multi-user eBook)

Printed in Guangzhou, China
1 2 3 4 5 6 7 8 9 0 28 27 26 25 24

052024
100923

Project Coordinator: John Willis
Designer: Jean Faye Rodriguez

Every reasonable effort has been made to trace ownership and to obtain permission to reprint copyright material. The publisher would be pleased to have any errors or omissions brought to its attention so that they may be corrected in subsequent printings.

The publisher acknowledges Getty Images and Shutterstock as the primary image suppliers for this title.

First published by BookLife in 2018